Presidents of the United States Bio-Graphics

Ronald Reagan
40th U.S. President

40

Written by **Joeming Dunn**   Illustrated by **Ben Dunn**

visit us at www.abdopublishing.com

Published by Magic Wagon, a division of the ABDO Publishing Group, 8000 West 78th Street, Edina, Minnesota 55439. Copyright © 2012 by Abdo Consulting Group, Inc. International copyrights reserved in all countries. All rights reserved. No part of this book may be reproduced in any form without written permission from the publisher.

Graphic Planet™ is a trademark and logo of Magic Wagon.

Printed in the United States of America, North Mankato, Minnesota.
042011
092011
This book contains at least 10% recycled materials.

Written by Joeming Dunn
Illustrated by Ben Dunn
Colored by Robby Bevard
Lettered by Doug Dlin
Edited by Stephanie Hedlund and Rochelle Baltzer
Interior layout and design by Antarctic Press
Cover art by Ben Dunn
Cover design by Abbey Fitzgerald

Library of Congress Cataloging-in-Publication Data

Dunn, Joeming W.
   Ronald Reagan : 40th U.S. president / written by Joeming Dunn ; illustrated by Ben Dunn.
      p. cm.
   Includes index.
   ISBN 978-1-61641-649-2
   1. Reagan, Ronald--Juvenile literature. 2. Presidents--United States--Biography--Juvenile literature. I. Dunn, Ben. II. Title.
   E877.D87 2012
   973.927092--dc22

   [B]

30007002116704

2011011049

Table of Contents

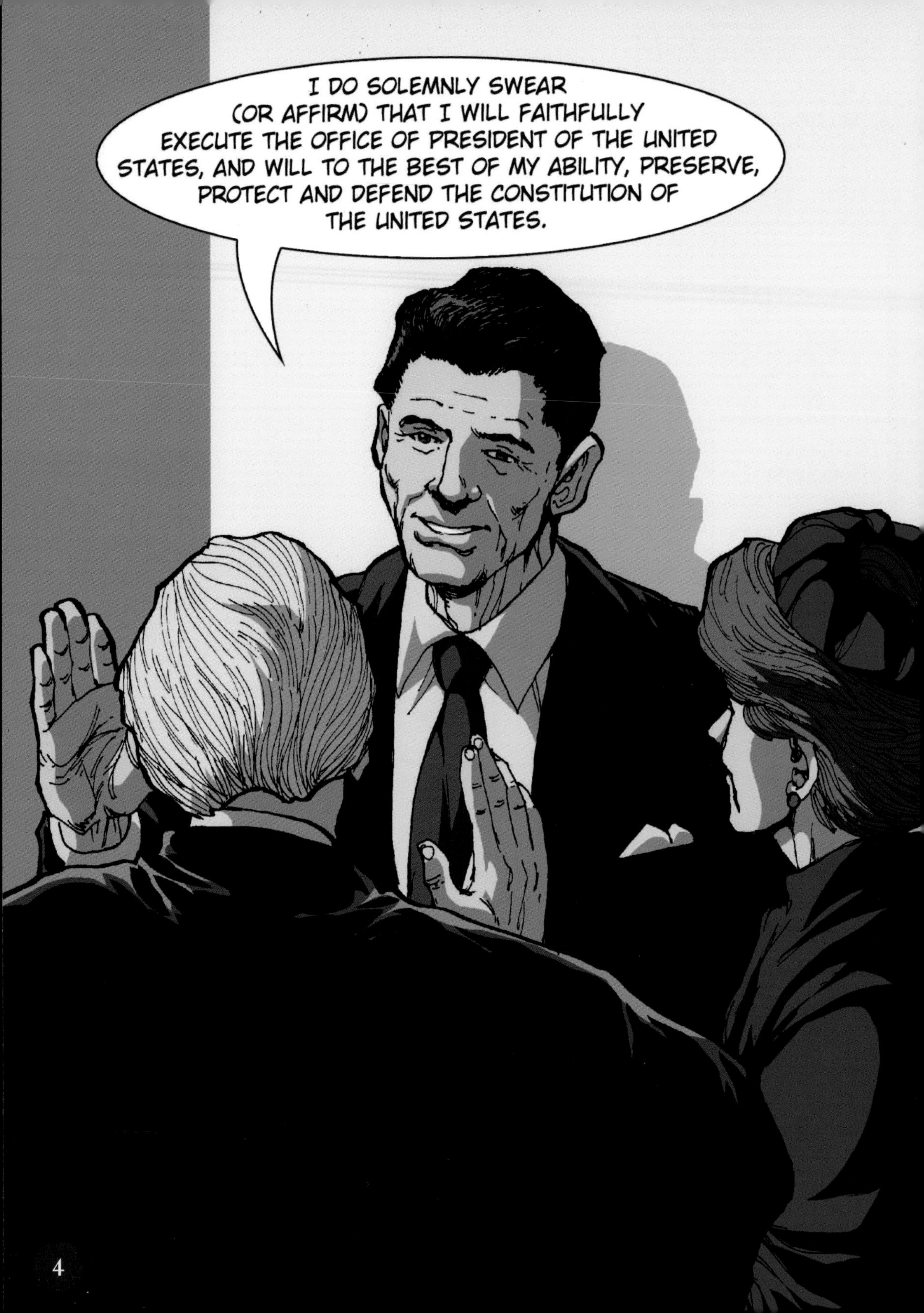
I DO SOLEMNLY SWEAR (OR AFFIRM) THAT I WILL FAITHFULLY EXECUTE THE OFFICE OF PRESIDENT OF THE UNITED STATES, AND WILL TO THE BEST OF MY ABILITY, PRESERVE, PROTECT AND DEFEND THE CONSTITUTION OF THE UNITED STATES.

Chapter 1:
Young Reagan

HE LOOKS LIKE A FAT LITTLE DUTCHMAN. WE'LL CALL HIM DUTCH.

Ronald Wilson Reagan was born in Tampico, Illinois, on February 6, 1911. His parents were Nelle Wilson and Jack Reagan. He had an older brother named Neil.

The family moved many times. In 1920, they settled in Dixon, Illinois.

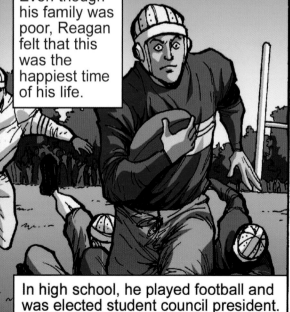

Even though his family was poor, Reagan felt that this was the happiest time of his life.

In high school, he played football and was elected student council president.

After high school, Reagan attended Eureka College in Eureka, Illinois. He graduated in 1932.

EUREKA COLLEGE
Chartered 1855

He soon landed a job as a radio announcer in Davenport, Iowa. Then he moved and began working at WHO in Des Moines, Iowa. There, he mostly did sportscasting.

AND IT'S A BASE HIT TO RIGHT FIELD...

After college, Reagan began looking for a job.

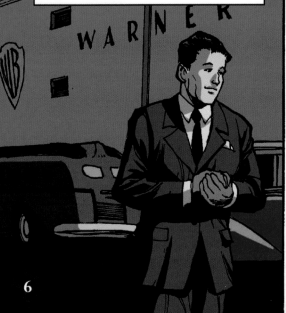

In 1937, he was sent to report on the Chicago Cubs spring training in California. While there, Reagan got a screen test at Warner Brothers Studios.

Warner Brothers immediately signed him to a contract.

WIN ONE FOR THE GIPPER.

Reagan's first movie was *Love Is on the Air*. He played a radio announcer.

Over the next 27 years, he starred in more than 50 films. His most memorable film was *Knute Rockne: All American*. In it, he played dying football player George Gipp.

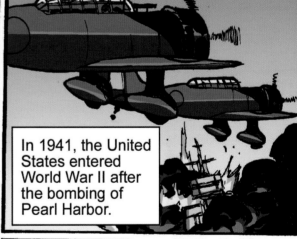

In 1941, the United States entered World War II after the bombing of Pearl Harbor.

Reagan was a member of the reserve. So he was called up to active duty. But a medical condition made him unable to fight.

While filming the movie *Brother Rat*, he met costar Jane Wyman. They fell in love and married in 1940. They had two children together.

Instead, he made training films for the military.

7

In 1947, Reagan was elected president of the Screen Actors Guild. This is a labor union for film actors.

During this time, Reagan helped Congress blacklist several actors, writers, and directors. He did this because they supposedly favored communism.

Reagan was a Democrat. He supported Harry Truman in the election of 1948. But, his feelings began to change about politics.

Then in 1949, Jane divorced him. To this day, Reagan is the only president ever to have been divorced.

In 1949, Reagan met an actress named Nancy Davis. They were married in 1952. Together they had two children.

Reagan began to disagree with some of the Democrats' ideas. In 1950, he supported Republican Richard Nixon in his senatorial campaign.

Reagan was a tireless campaigner. He delivered many speeches in support of the Republican Party.

In 1954, Reagan became the host of a television series called *General Electric Theater*. He also became a spokesman for General Electric.

He toured the country and gave speeches.

I DO BELIEVE WE ARE OVERBURDENED WITH TAXES...

In 1962, Reagan officially changed parties and registered as a Republican.

9

Reagan continued to support Republican candidates. In 1964, he gave a 30-minute, nationally televised speech called "A Time for Choosing."

YOU AND I HAVE A RENDEZVOUS WITH DESTINY.

As a result of the speech, hundreds of thousands of dollars were given to the Barry Goldwater presidential campaign. Some say it was one of the most successful political speeches in history.

Reagan used his success to run for California governor in 1966.

RONALD REAGAN FOR GOVERNOR

He was running against the current governor, Edmund G. Brown. Brown said Reagan lacked experience.

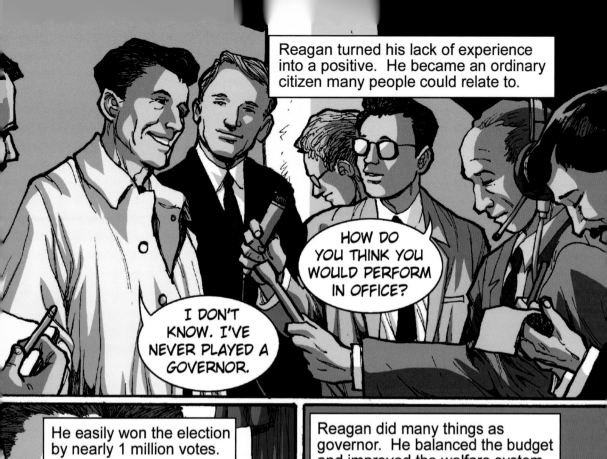

Reagan turned his lack of experience into a positive. He became an ordinary citizen many people could relate to.

HOW DO YOU THINK YOU WOULD PERFORM IN OFFICE?

I DON'T KNOW. I'VE NEVER PLAYED A GOVERNOR.

He easily won the election by nearly 1 million votes.

REAGA for GOVERNO

Reagan did many things as governor. He balanced the budget and improved the welfare system. He served two terms as governor, holding office until 1974.

In 1974, Richard Nixon gave up his position as president due to the Watergate scandal. Vice President Gerald Ford replaced him.

REPUBLICAN NATIONAL CONVENTION 1974

Reagan saw Ford was losing popularity with the American people. So, Reagan tried to get the Republican nomination for president in 1976.

SOLD

HOUSE FOR SALE

Reagan lost the nomination by just a few votes. After the loss, he spent the next four years managing real estate investments.

He was also preparing for his next move. He was going to run in the presidential election of 1980.

Reagan easily received the Republican nomination for president in 1980.

During the primaries, he chose George Herbert Walker Bush as his running mate.

Reagan and Bush ran on a platform of reducing taxes, increasing defense spending, and balancing the budget.

It would be a tough road ahead. They were campaigning against President Jimmy Carter and Vice President Walter Mondale.

During the campaign, Reagan often focused on Carter's weaknesses.

ARE YOU BETTER OFF THAN YOU WERE FOUR YEARS AGO?

13

Reagan pointed out that unemployment, inflation, and interest rates were rising.

He talked about how President Carter had failed to resolve the Iranian hostage crisis. In November 1979, Iranian students stormed the U.S. embassy and took the staff hostage. It became worse after a failed rescue mission.

Many thought it was going to be a close race, but it ended in a Reagan landslide victory. Reagan became the 40th president of the United States. His inauguration speech included the announcement of the release of the hostages in Iran.

On March 30, 1981, John W. Hinckley Jr. shot and wounded President Reagan.

Even after being shot, Reagan kept his sense of humor. He quickly recovered from his wounds.

I HOPE YOU'RE ALL REPUBLICANS.

TODAY, MR. PRESIDENT, WE'RE ALL REPUBLICANS.

Reagan was soon back to work. In August 1981, the air traffic controllers went on strike. They were demanding better pay and benefits.

ON STRIKE!

STRIKE!

STRIKE!

Reagan declared the strike was illegal. He fired them all and replaced them with military controllers until new controllers could be trained.

NOTICE
TERMINATION OF EMPLOYMENT
YOU ARE FIRED!!

In the early 1980s, the country was in a recession. Many people were unemployed and there was high interest rates and high inflation.

UNEMPLOYMENT OFFICE

Reagan claimed the government was getting too big and taxes were too high. He said the country needed to change.

WALL ST.

Reagan wanted to reduce government spending, income tax, government regulation, and inflation. He pushed this economic policy, which became known as Reaganomics.

Reagan's policies were successful in creating wealth. But some people claimed they would only help the rich.

The idea was that if you gave growth to the top, it would eventually go to the bottom, or "trickle down."

Reagan's policies did create jobs and the economy recovered. But, many manufacturing jobs were lost.

It also greatly increased the national debt.

Reagan appointed many judges during his political career. He was the first president to appoint a woman to the Supreme Court. That woman was Sandra Day O'Connor.

Reagan also believed in a strong military. He increased the military budgets.

He was anti-communist and especially anti-Soviet Union. Reagan felt a strong military was needed for protection.

THE SOVIET UNION IS AN EVIL EMPIRE, THE FOCUS OF EVIL IN THE MODERN WORLD.

Part of the military buildup was the Strategic Defense Initiative, or "Star Wars" project.

This project created a special system to destroy enemy missiles in flight.

Some say the U.S. military growth forced the Soviets to the bargaining table. This resulted in a treaty that reduced the number of nuclear missiles.

The treaty was the beginning of a period of openness in the Soviet Union.

MR. GORBECHEV, TEAR DOWN THIS WALL.

This led to the fall of the Berlin Wall. The Soviet Union broke up soon after.

Chapter 7:
Troubled Times

Even though he kept the United States out of any foreign wars, Reagan's Administration was involved in many troublesome areas.

In 1979, the Soviet Union invaded Afghanistan.

The United States supplied money and military equipment to Afghan rebels to fight the government. This led to the withdrawal of the Soviet Union in 1989.

Many argue that U.S. and Soviet intervention allowed the present-day Taliban and Osama Bin Laden to have a safe place in Afghanistan.

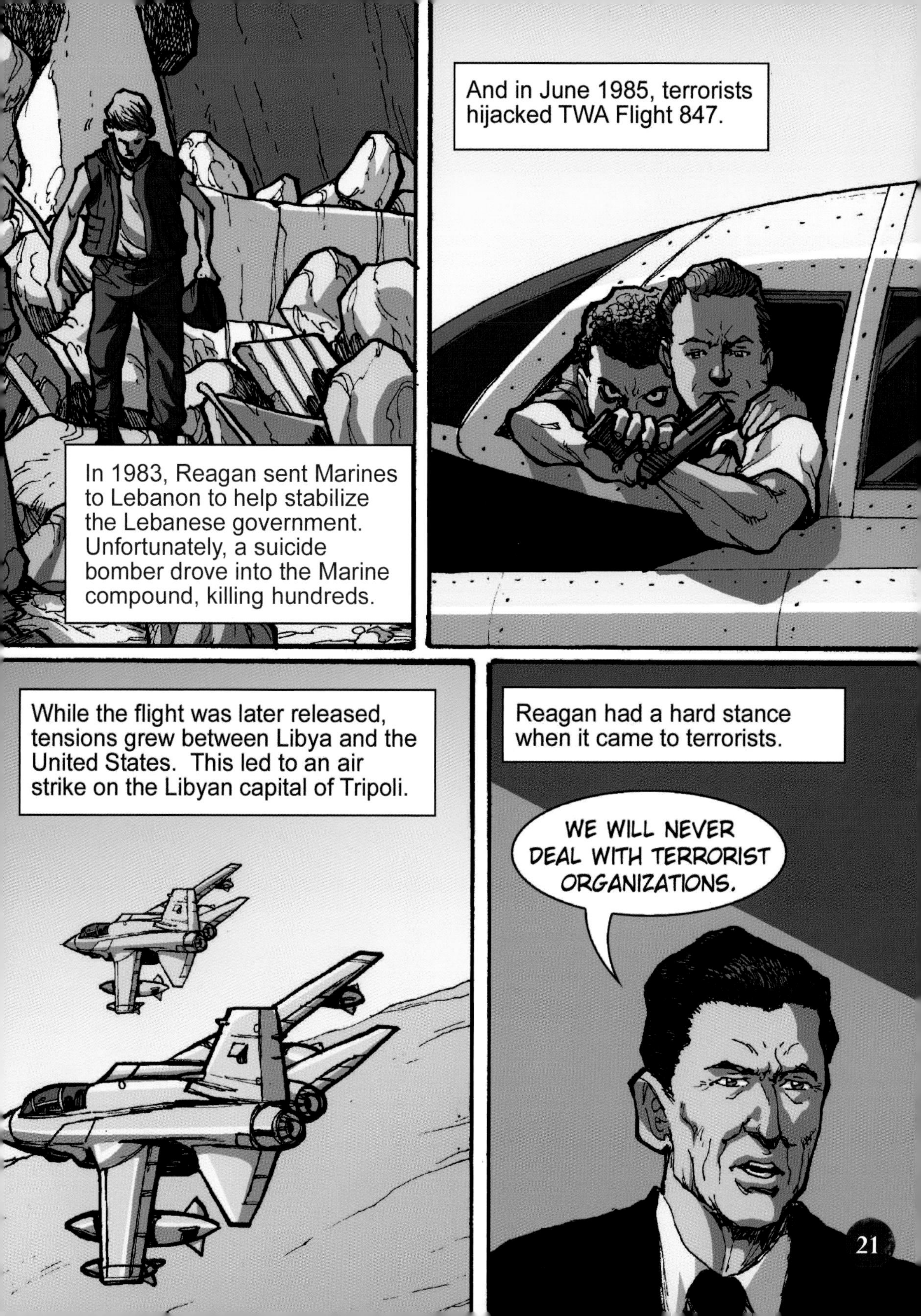
In 1983, Reagan sent Marines to Lebanon to help stabilize the Lebanese government. Unfortunately, a suicide bomber drove into the Marine compound, killing hundreds.
And in June 1985, terrorists hijacked TWA Flight 847.
While the flight was later released, tensions grew between Libya and the United States. This led to an air strike on the Libyan capital of Tripoli.
Reagan had a hard stance when it came to terrorists.
WE WILL NEVER DEAL WITH TERRORIST ORGANIZATIONS.

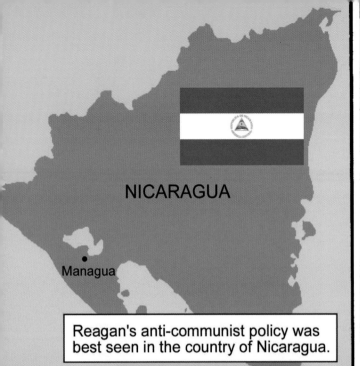

NICARAGUA

• Managua

Reagan's anti-communist policy was best seen in the country of Nicaragua.

In 1979, the Sandinista National Liberation Front overthrew the government. It was controlled by the Somoza dictatorship.

VIVA LA REVOLUCION

The Reagan Administration gave arms and weapons to the Somozan rebels, called Contras. While they were few in number, the Contras caused much damage to Nicaragua.

In 1984, the Bowland Amendment was passed. This amendment stopped aid to the Contras.

In the 1984 presidential election, Reagan and Bush easily defeated Walter Mondale and Geraldine Ferraro. Reagan received 525 electoral votes to Mondale's 13. This made Reagan's total the largest number of electoral votes in presidential election history.

Early in his second term, Reagan was involved in a scandal.

The New York Times

"All the News That's Fit to Print"

VOL.CXXXVI...No. 46,978   NEW YORK, WEDNESDAY, NOVEMBER 26, 1986   30 CENTS

IRAN PAYMENT FOUND DIVERTED TO CONTRAS; REAGAN SECURITY ADVISER AND AIDE ARE OUT

Friedman Is Guilty With 3 in Scandal

DISARRAY DEEPENS

Was Not 'Fully Informed' About Secret Moves.

Reagan approved the sale of arms to Iran for the release of hostages still held in Lebanon. This sale didn't follow the policy against aiding countries that supported terrorists.

It was soon discovered that part of the money earned from the sale was sent to a secret fund that supplied the Contras in Nicaragua. This was a violation of the Bowland Amendment.

NICARAGUA

IRAN

Lieutenant Colonel Oliver North was said to be in charge of sending the funds to the Contras.

A special commission was appointed to look into the matter. It was headed by former Senator John Tower. North was later fired from his position.

Reagan denied involvement in the scandal. But, he accepted responsibility for the actions of his staff members.

Even with the scandal, Reagan's popularity among Americans remained high.

One of Reagan's last acts as president was to help Vice President George H.W. Bush get the Republican nomination for president. Bush defeated Democratic challenger Michael Dukakis.

Reagan then retired to his ranch in Los Angeles.

In 1990, he released an autobiography called *An American Life*. It was an instant best seller.

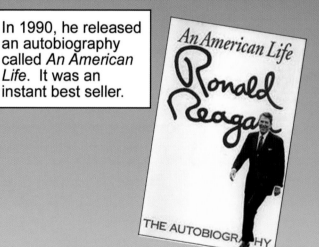

He also remained a very popular speaker.

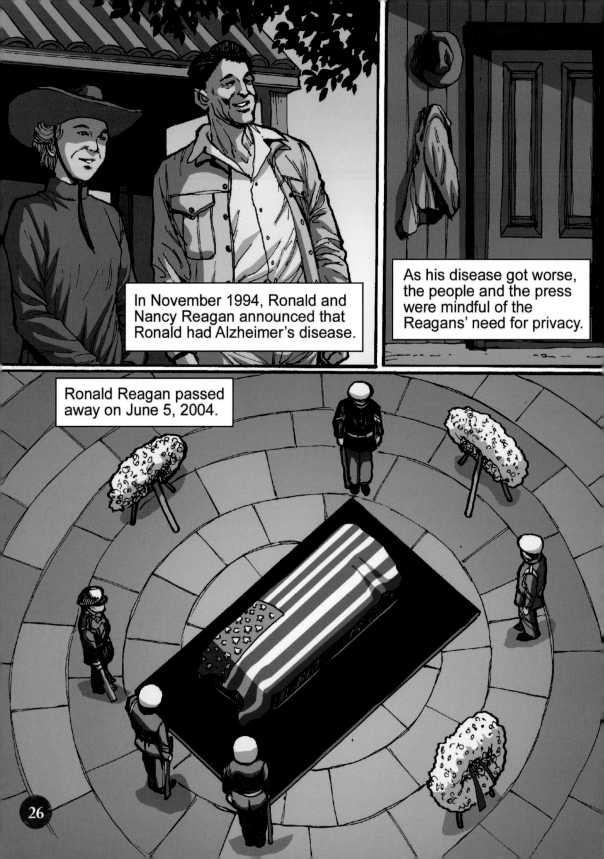

In November 1994, Ronald and Nancy Reagan announced that Ronald had Alzheimer's disease.

As his disease got worse, the people and the press were mindful of the Reagans' need for privacy.

Ronald Reagan passed away on June 5, 2004.

In 1993, Reagan was honored with the Presidential Medal of Freedom, the highest honor the United States can give. In 1998, Washington National Airport in Washington DC was renamed Ronald Reagan National Airport.

And in 1999, the aircraft carrier *USS Ronald Reagan* was named by Nancy Reagan. To this day, Ronald Reagan remains one of the most popular presidents in U.S. history.

Fast Facts

Name - Ronald Reagan   Born - February 6, 1911

Wives - Jane Wyman (1917–2007), Nancy Davis (1921–)   Children - 4

Political Party - Republican

Age at Inauguration - 69   Years Served - 1981–1989

Vice President - George H.W. Bush

Died - June 5, 2004, age 93

President Reagan's Cabinet

First term - January 20, 1981 -
January 20, 1985

State – Alexander Haig Jr.; George P. Shultz (from July 16, 1982)

Treasury – Donald T. Regan

Defense – Caspar Weinberger

Attorney General – William French Smith

Interior – James G. Watt; William P. Clark (from November 21, 1983)

Agriculture – John R. Block

Commerce – Malcolm Baldrige

Labor – Raymond J. Donovan

Health and human services – Richard S. Schweiker; Margaret M. Heckler (from March 9, 1983)

Housing and Urban Development – Samuel R. Pierce Jr.

Transportation – Andrew L. Lewis Jr.; Elizabeth H. Dole (from February 7, 1983)

Energy – James B. Edwards; Donald P. Hodel (from December 8, 1982)

Education – Terrel H. Bell

Second term - January 20, 1985 -
January 20, 1989

State – George P. Shultz

Second term Continued

Treasury – Donald T. Regan; James A. Baker III (from February 25, 1985); Nicholas F. Brady (from August 18, 1988)

Defense – Caspar Weinberger; Frank Carlucci (from November 21, 1987)

Attorney General – William French Smith; Edwin Meese (from February 25, 1985); Dick Thornburgh (from August 11, 1988)

Interior – Donald P. Hodel

Agriculture – John R. Block; Richard E. Lyng (from March 7, 1986)

Commerce – Malcolm Baldrige; C. William Verity (from October 19, 1987)

Labor – Raymond J. Donovan; William E. Brock (from April 29, 1985); Ann McLaughlin (from December 17, 1987)

Health and human services – Margaret M. Heckler; Otis R. Bowen (from December 13, 1985)

Housing and Urban Development – Samuel R. Pierce Jr.

Transportation – Elizabeth H. Dole; James H. Burnley (from December 3, 1987)

Energy – John S. Herrington

Education – Terrel H. Bell; William J. Bennett (from February 7, 1985); Lauro F. Cavazos (from September 20, 1988)

• To be president, a person must meet three requirements. He or she must be at least 35 years old and a natural-born U.S. citizen. A candidate must also have lived in the United States for at least 14 years.

• The U.S. presidential election is an indirect election. Voters from each state elect representatives called electors for the Electoral College. The number of electors is based on population. Each elector pledges to cast their vote for the candidate who receives the highest number of popular votes in their state. A candidate must receive the majority of Electoral College votes to win.

• Each president may be elected to two four-year terms. The presidential election is held on the Tuesday after the first Monday in November. The president is sworn in on January 20 of the following year.

• While in office, the president receives a salary of $400,000 each year. He or she lives in the White House and has 24-hour Secret Service protection. When the president leaves office, he or she receives Secret Service protection for ten more years. He or she also receives a yearly pension of $191,300 and funding for office space, supplies, and staff.

Timeline

1911 - Ronald Reagan was born on February 6.

1932 - Reagan graduated from Eureka College.

1937 - Reagan's acting career began with Warner Brothers Studios.

1940 - Reagan married Jane Wyman.

1942 - Reagan entered the military.

1947 - Reagan became president of the Screen Actors Guild.

1949 - Reagan and Jane Wyman divorced.

1952 - Reagan married Nancy Davis.

1966 - Reagan was elected governor of California.

1980 - Reagan was elected the fortieth U.S. president.

1981 - Reagan took office on January 20; on March 30 Reagan survived an assassination attempt by John W. Hinckley Jr.

1984 - Reagan was reelected president by the biggest margin in U.S. history.

1987 - Reagan gave a speech at Berlin Wall on June 12.

1993 - Reagan received the Presidential Medal of Freedom.

2004 - Ronald Reagan died on June 5.

Web Sites

To learn more about Ronald Reagan, visit ABDO Publishing Group online at **www.abdopublishing.com**. Web sites about Reagan are featured on our Book Links page. These links are routinely monitored and updated to provide the most current information available.

Glossary

Administration - the people who manage a presidential government.

Alzheimer's disease - an illness that causes forgetfulness, confusion, and overall mental disintegration.

Berlin Wall - a physical barrier that separated East Berlin, German Democratic Republic, and West Berlin, West Germany, from 1961 to 1989.

blacklist - a list of persons who are disapproved of or boycotted.

campaign - to give speeches and state ideas in order to be voted into an elected office.

communism - a social and economic system in which everything is owned by the government and given to the people as needed. A person who believes in communism is called a communist.

Democrat - a member of the Democratic political party. Democrats believe in social change and strong government.

hijack - to take over an airplane by threatening violence.

hostage - a person captured by another person or group in order to make a deal with authorities.

inauguration - a ceremony in which a person is sworn into a political office.

inflation - a rise in the price of goods and services.

labor union - a group of workers formed to protect their interests, such as wages and working conditions.

nomination - the act of choosing a candidate for election

platform - a statement of the principles of a politician or a political party.

primary - a method of selecting candidates to run for public office. A political party holds an election among its own members. They select the party members who will represent it in the coming general election.

recession - a time when business activity slows.

Republican - a member of the Republican political party. Republicans are conservative and believe in small government.

running mate - a candidate running for a lower-rank position on an election ticket, especially the candidate for vice president.

scandal - an action that shocks people and disgraces those connected with it.

screen test - filming a small part of a movie to see if a person is right for a role.

Taliban - a militia group in Afghanistan that follows the Islamic faith.

terrorist - a person who uses violence to threaten people or governments.

Index